SHARK ATTACK!

BETHANY HAMILTON'S STORY

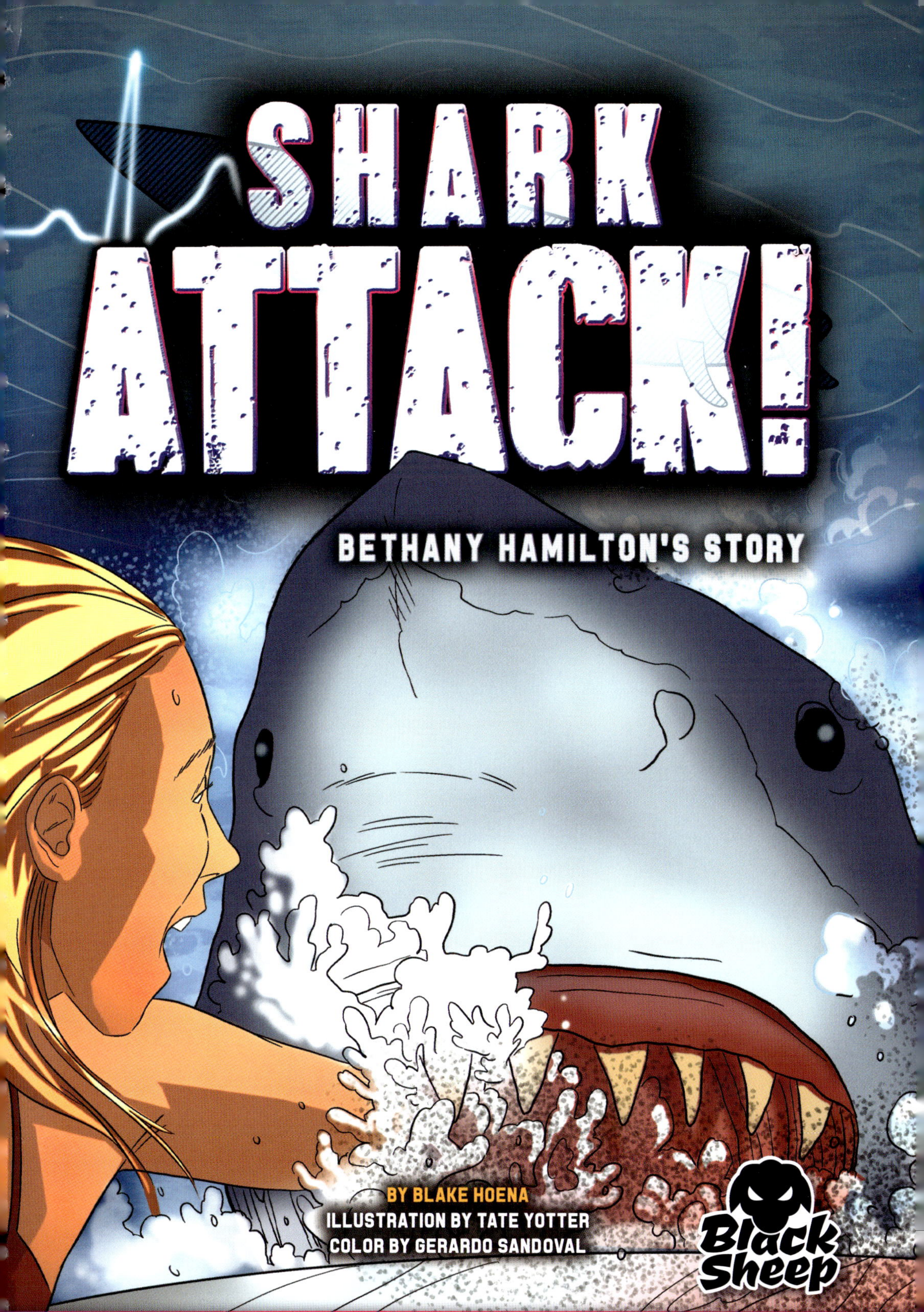

BY BLAKE HOENA
ILLUSTRATION BY TATE YOTTER
COLOR BY GERARDO SANDOVAL

Black Sheep
BELLWETHER MEDIA • MINNEAPOLIS, MN

STRAY FROM REGULAR READS WITH BLACK SHEEP BOOKS. FEEL A RUSH WITH EVERY READ!

This edition first published in 2022 by Bellwether Media, Inc.

No part of this publication may be reproduced in whole or in part without written permission of the publisher. For information regarding permission, write to Bellwether Media, Inc., Attention: Permissions Department, 6012 Blue Circle Drive, Minnetonka, MN 55343.

Library of Congress Cataloging-in-Publication Data

LC record for Shark Attack!: Bethany Hamilton's Story available at https://lccn.loc.gov/2021025036

Text copyright © 2022 by Bellwether Media, Inc. BLACK SHEEP and associated logos are trademarks and/or registered trademarks of Bellwether Media, Inc.

Editor: Betsy Rathburn   Designer: Andrea Schneider

Printed in the United States of America, North Mankato, MN.

TABLE OF CONTENTS

A BORN SURFER	4
SHARK ATTACK!	8
THE ROAD TO RECOVERY	16
MORE ABOUT BETHANY HAMILTON	22
GLOSSARY	23
TO LEARN MORE	24
INDEX	24

Red text identifies historical quotes.

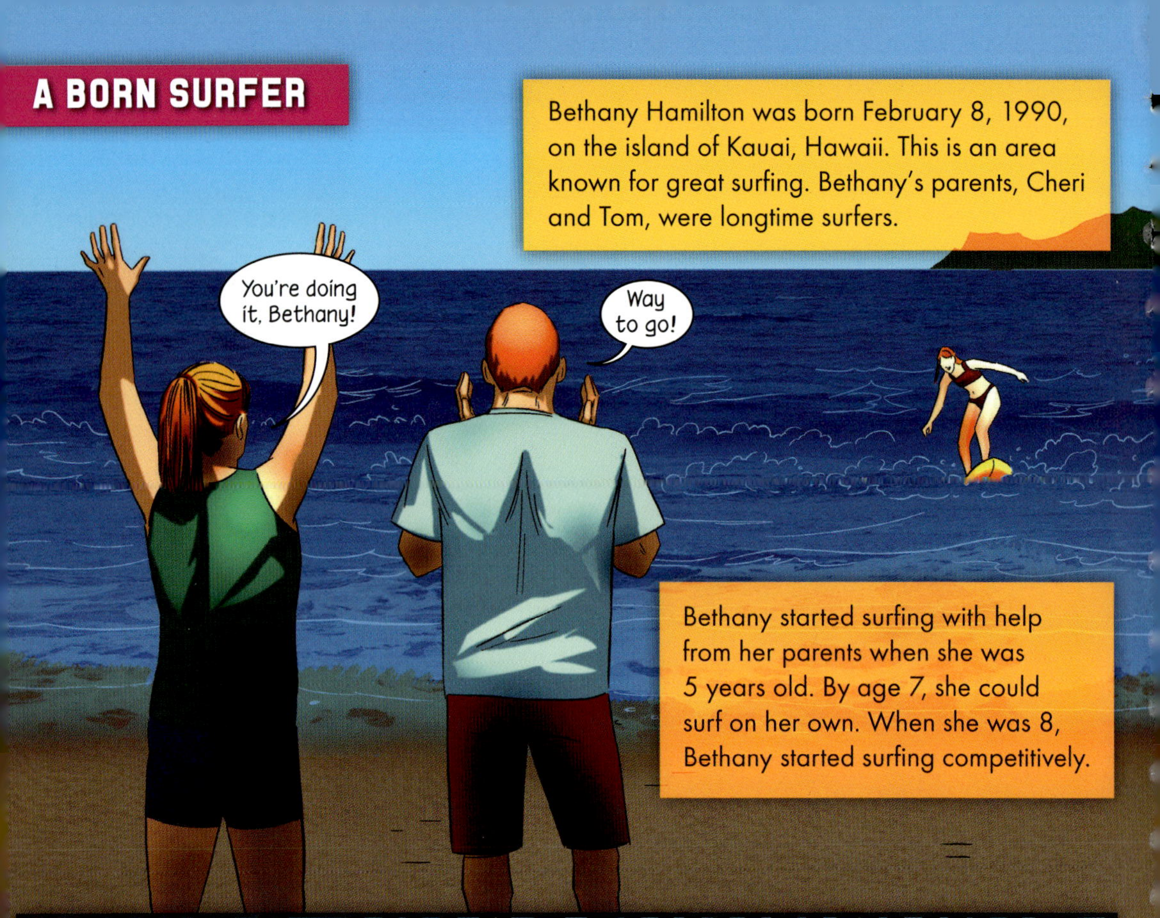
A BORN SURFER
Bethany Hamilton was born February 8, 1990, on the island of Kauai, Hawaii. This is an area known for great surfing. Bethany's parents, Cheri and Tom, were longtime surfers.
You're doing it, Bethany!
Way to go!
Bethany started surfing with help from her parents when she was 5 years old. By age 7, she could surf on her own. When she was 8, Bethany started surfing competitively.

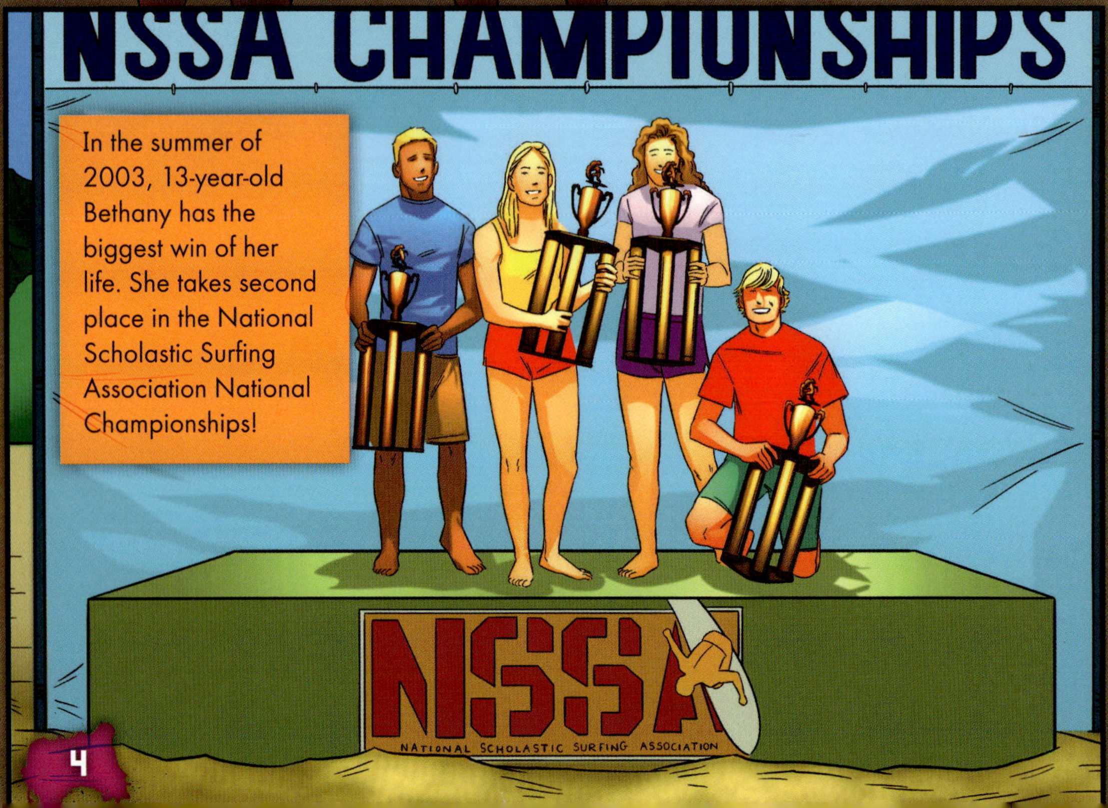
NSSA CHAMPIONSHIPS
In the summer of 2003, 13-year-old Bethany has the biggest win of her life. She takes second place in the National Scholastic Surfing Association National Championships!
NSSA
NATIONAL SCHOLASTIC SURFING ASSOCIATION

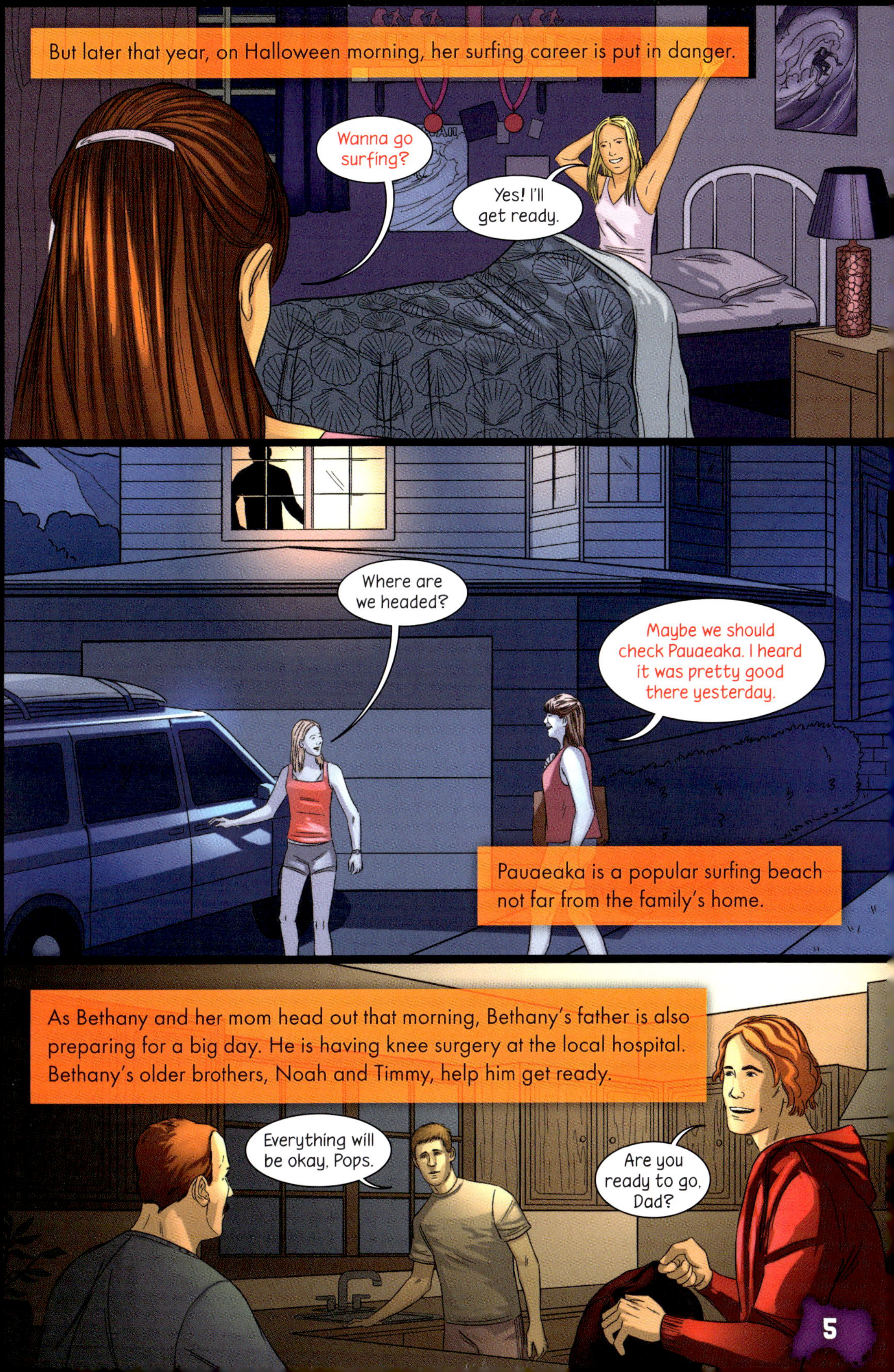
But later that year, on Halloween morning, her surfing career is put in danger.
Wanna go surfing?
Yes! I'll get ready.
Where are we headed?
Maybe we should check Pauaeaka. I heard it was pretty good there yesterday.
Pauaeaka is a popular surfing beach not far from the family's home.
As Bethany and her mom head out that morning, Bethany's father is also preparing for a big day. He is having knee surgery at the local hospital. Bethany's older brothers, Noah and Timmy, help him get ready.
Everything will be okay, Pops.
Are you ready to go, Dad?

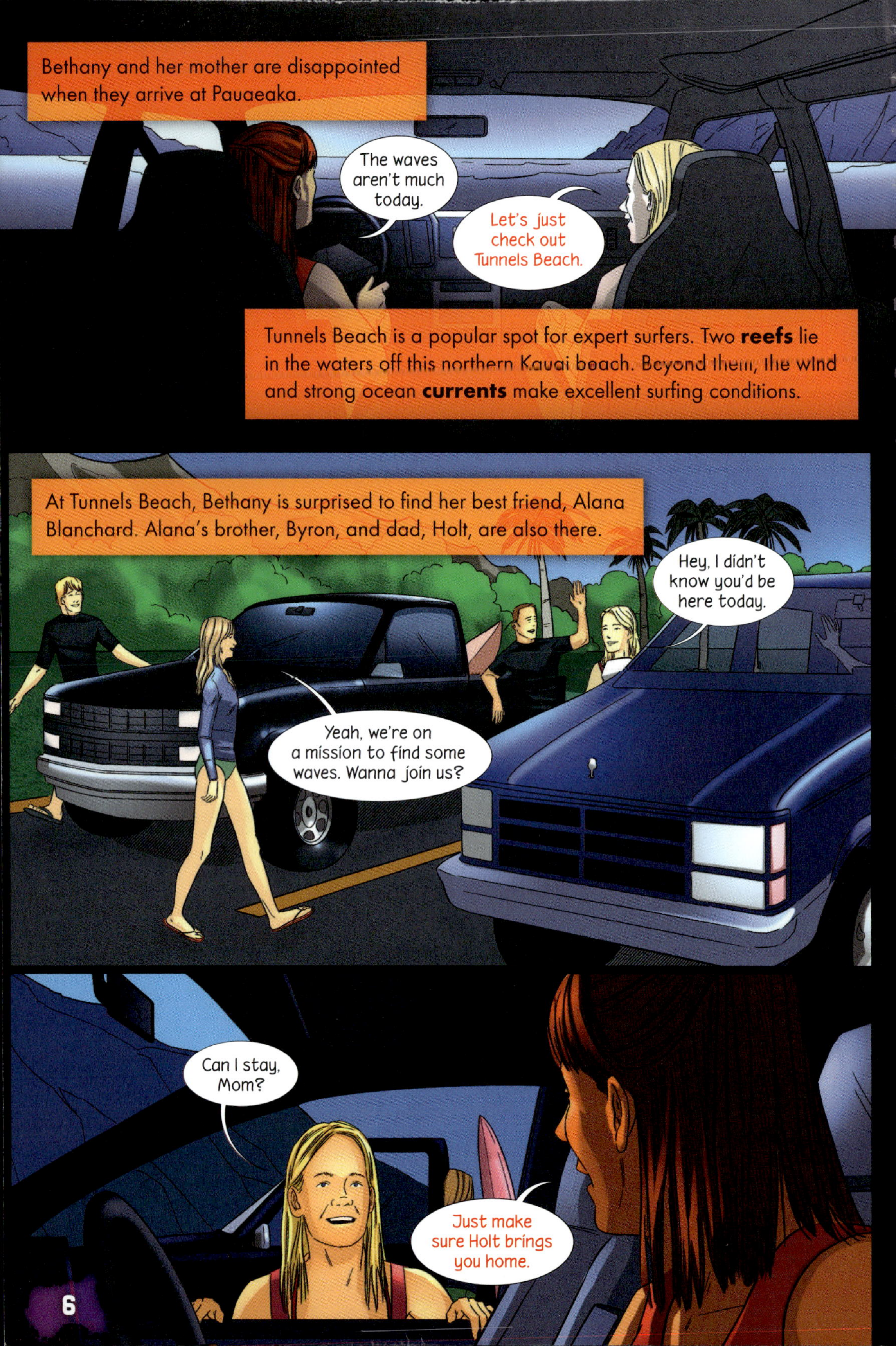

Bethany and her mother are disappointed when they arrive at Pauaeaka.
The waves aren't much today.
Let's just check out Tunnels Beach.
Tunnels Beach is a popular spot for expert surfers. Two **reefs** lie in the waters off this northern Kauai beach. Beyond them, the wind and strong ocean **currents** make excellent surfing conditions.
At Tunnels Beach, Bethany is surprised to find her best friend, Alana Blanchard. Alana's brother, Byron, and dad, Holt, are also there.
Hey, I didn't know you'd be here today.
Yeah, we're on a mission to find some waves. Wanna join us?
Can I stay, Mom?
Just make sure Holt brings you home.

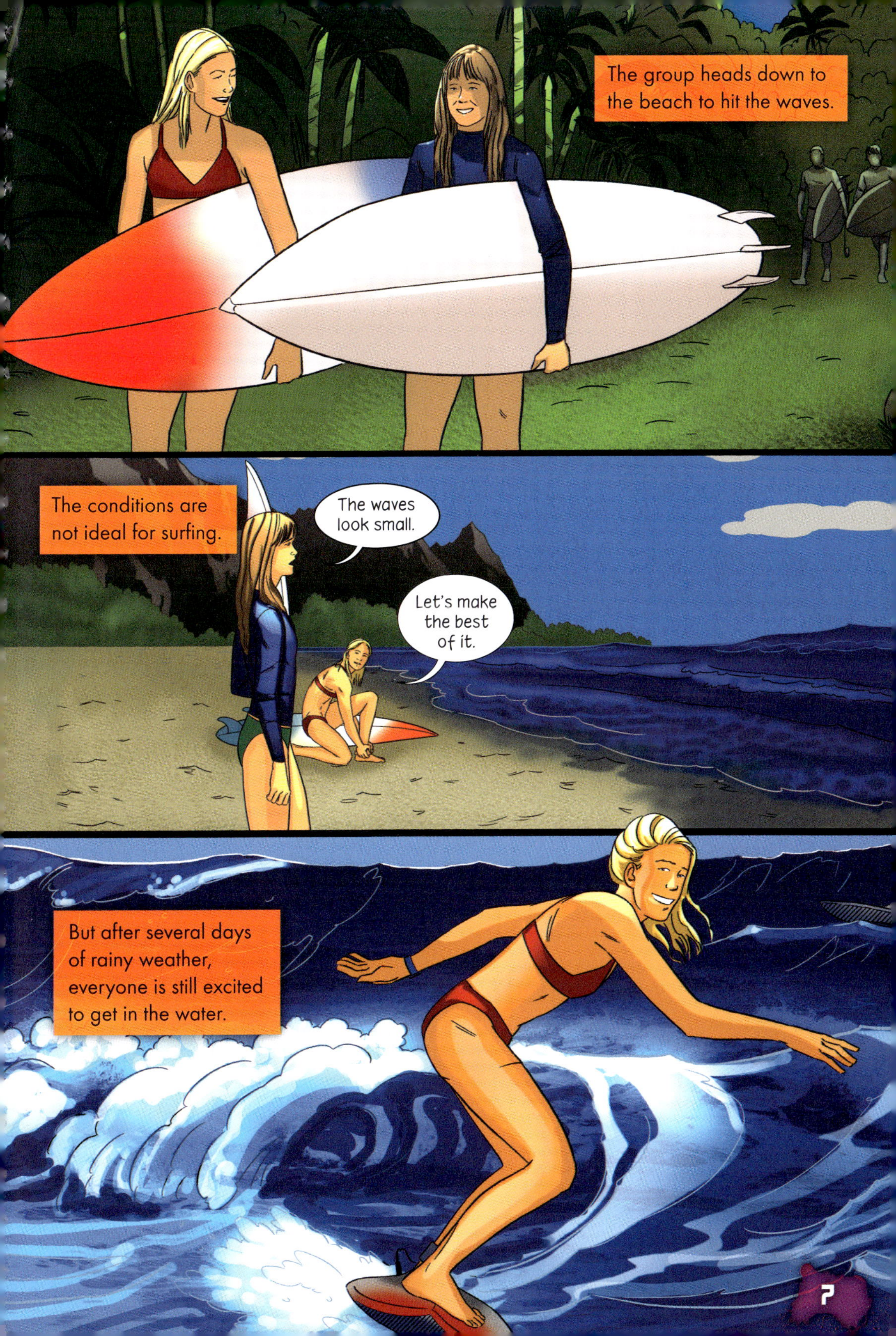
The group heads down to the beach to hit the waves.
The conditions are not ideal for surfing.
The waves look small.
Let's make the best of it.
But after several days of rainy weather, everyone is still excited to get in the water.

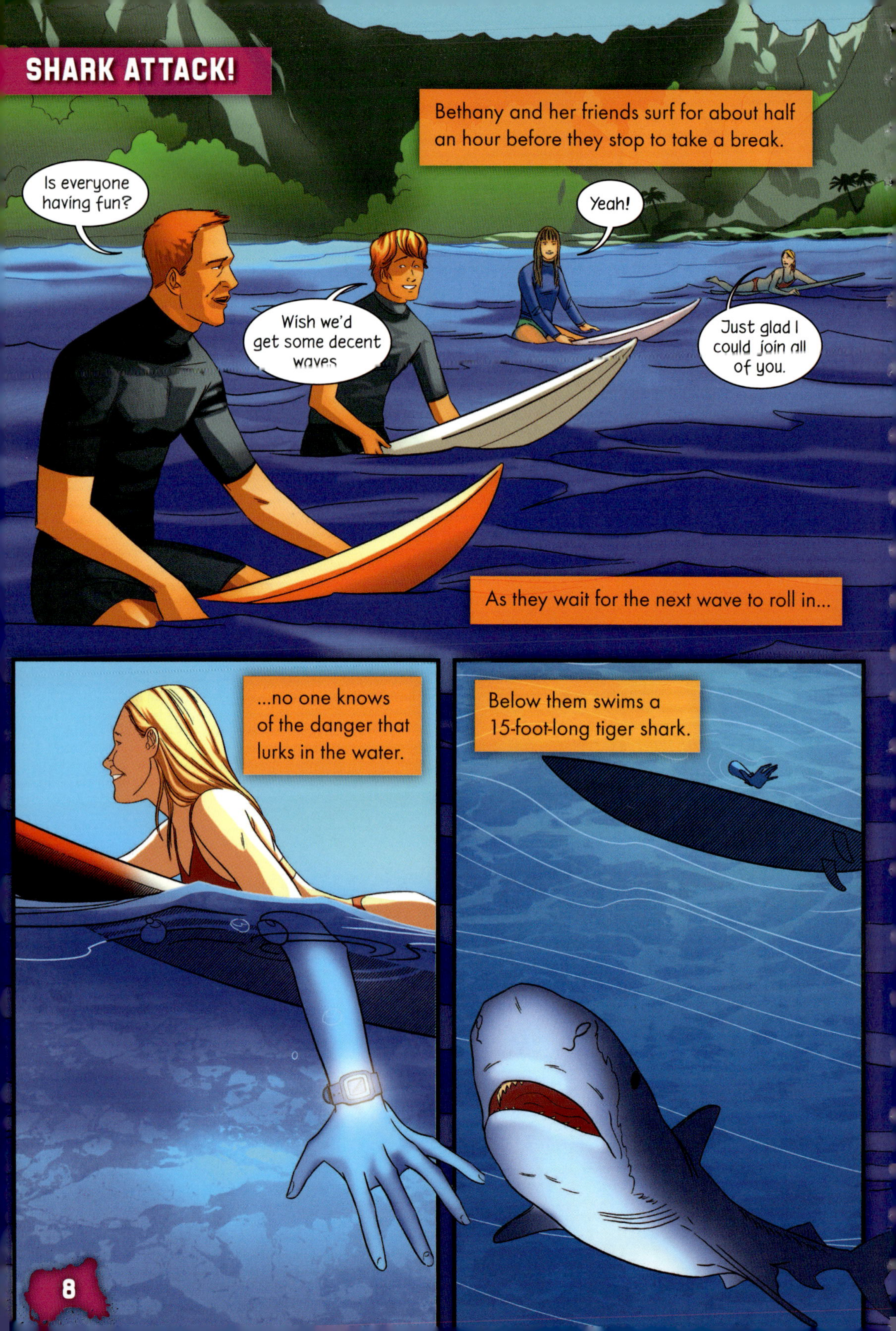
SHARK ATTACK!
Bethany and her friends surf for about half an hour before they stop to take a break.
Is everyone having fun?
Wish we'd get some decent waves
Yeah!
Just glad I could join all of you.
As they wait for the next wave to roll in...
...no one knows of the danger that lurks in the water.
Below them swims a 15-foot-long tiger shark.

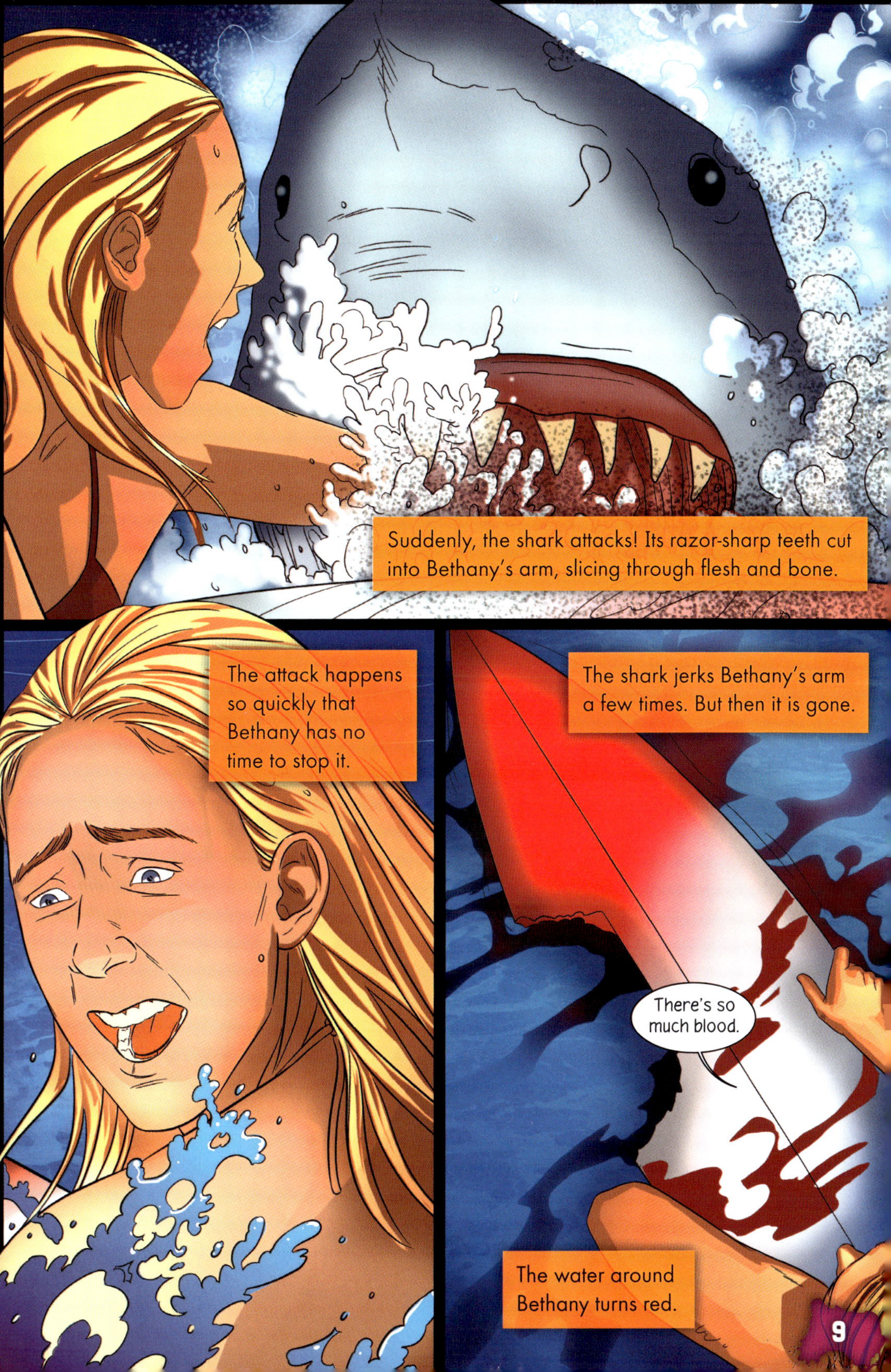
Suddenly, the shark attacks! Its razor-sharp teeth cut into Bethany's arm, slicing through flesh and bone.
The attack happens so quickly that Bethany has no time to stop it.
The shark jerks Bethany's arm a few times. But then it is gone.
There's so much blood.
The water around Bethany turns red.

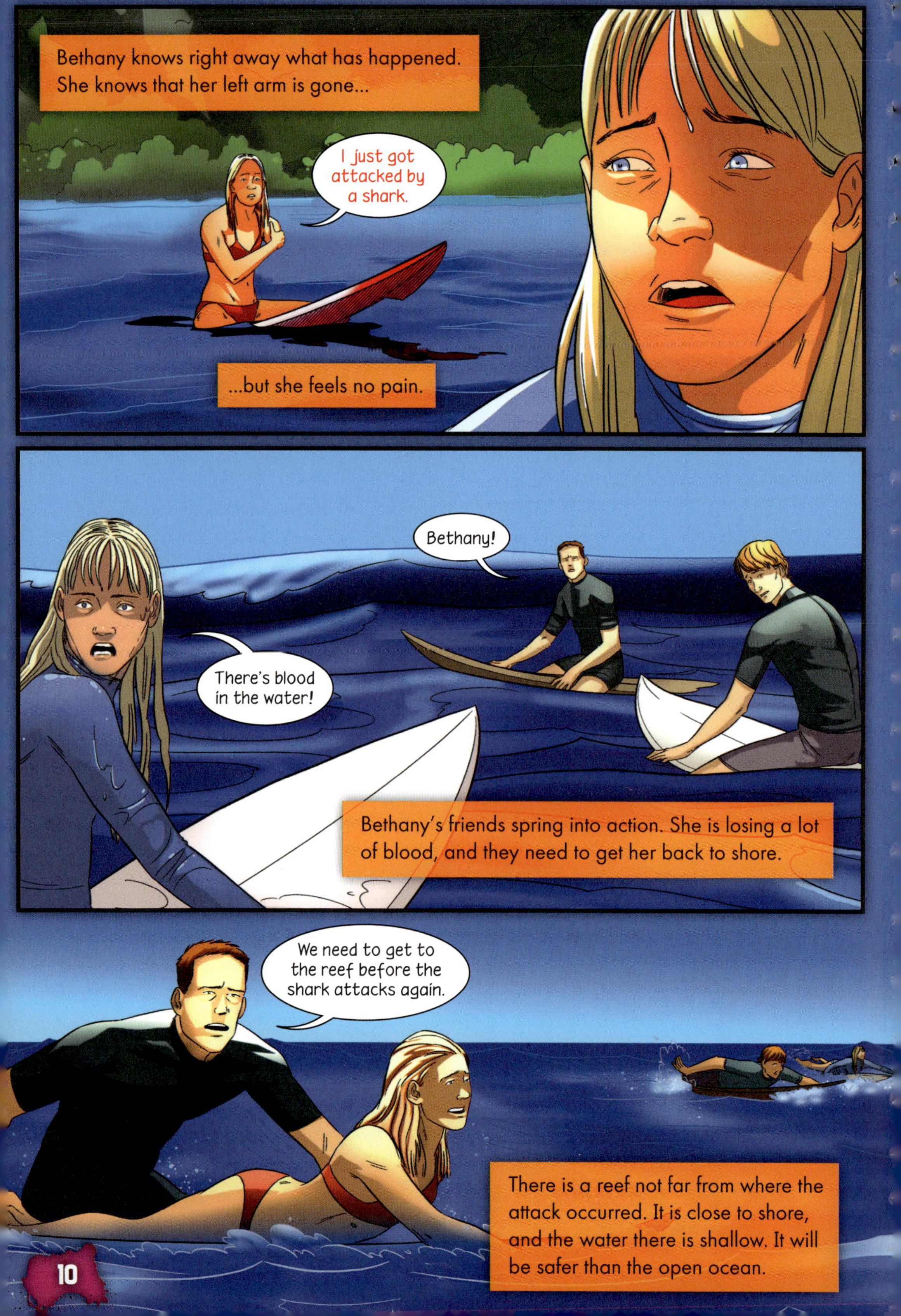

Bethany knows right away what has happened. She knows that her left arm is gone...
I just got attacked by a shark.
...but she feels no pain.
Bethany!
There's blood in the water!
Bethany's friends spring into action. She is losing a lot of blood, and they need to get her back to shore.
We need to get to the reef before the shark attacks again.
There is a reef not far from where the attack occurred. It is close to shore, and the water there is shallow. It will be safer than the open ocean.

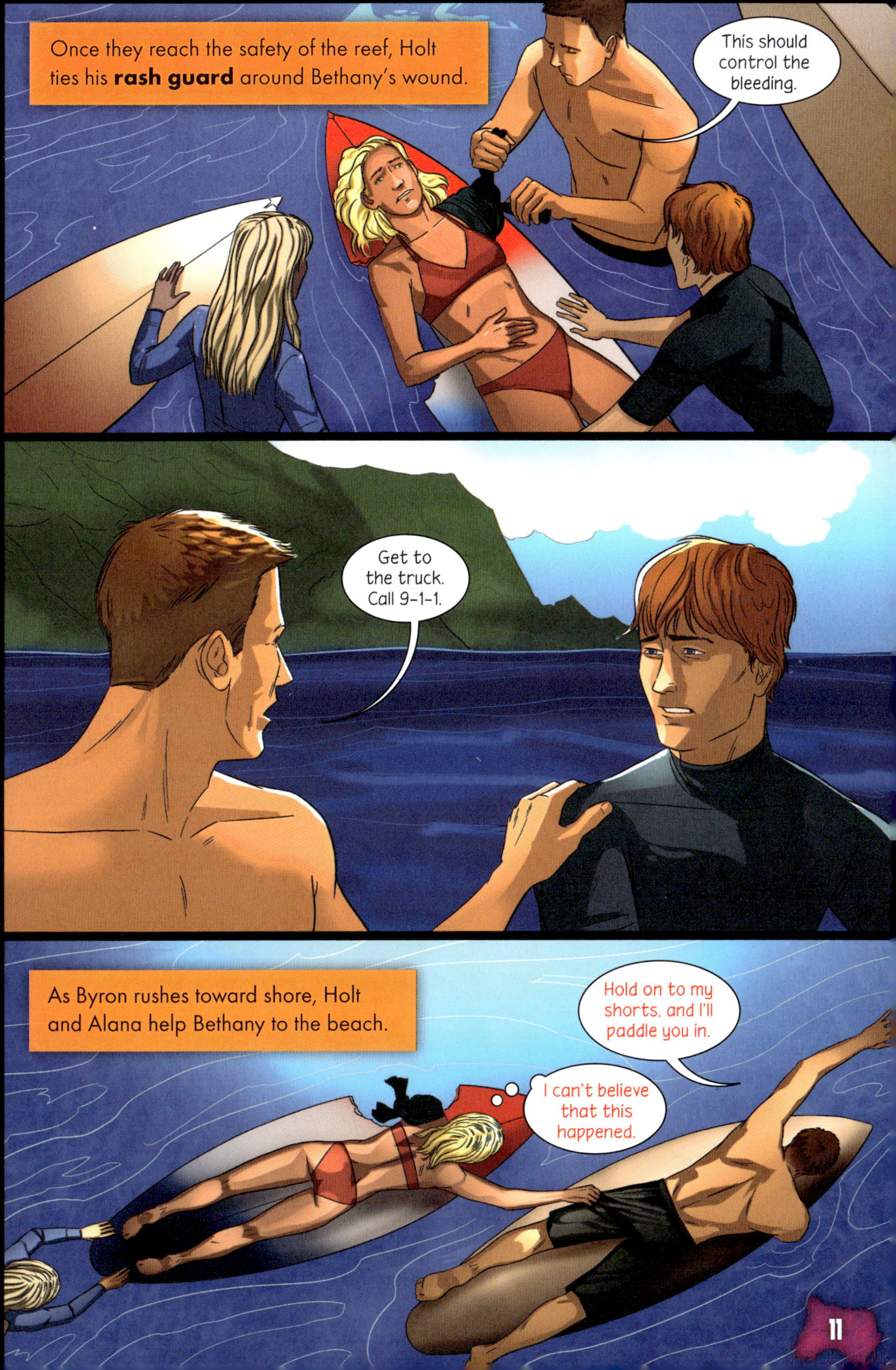
Once they reach the safety of the reef, Holt ties his **rash guard** around Bethany's wound.
This should control the bleeding.
Get to the truck. Call 9-1-1.
As Byron rushes toward shore, Holt and Alana help Bethany to the beach.
Hold on to my shorts, and I'll paddle you in.
I can't believe that this happened.

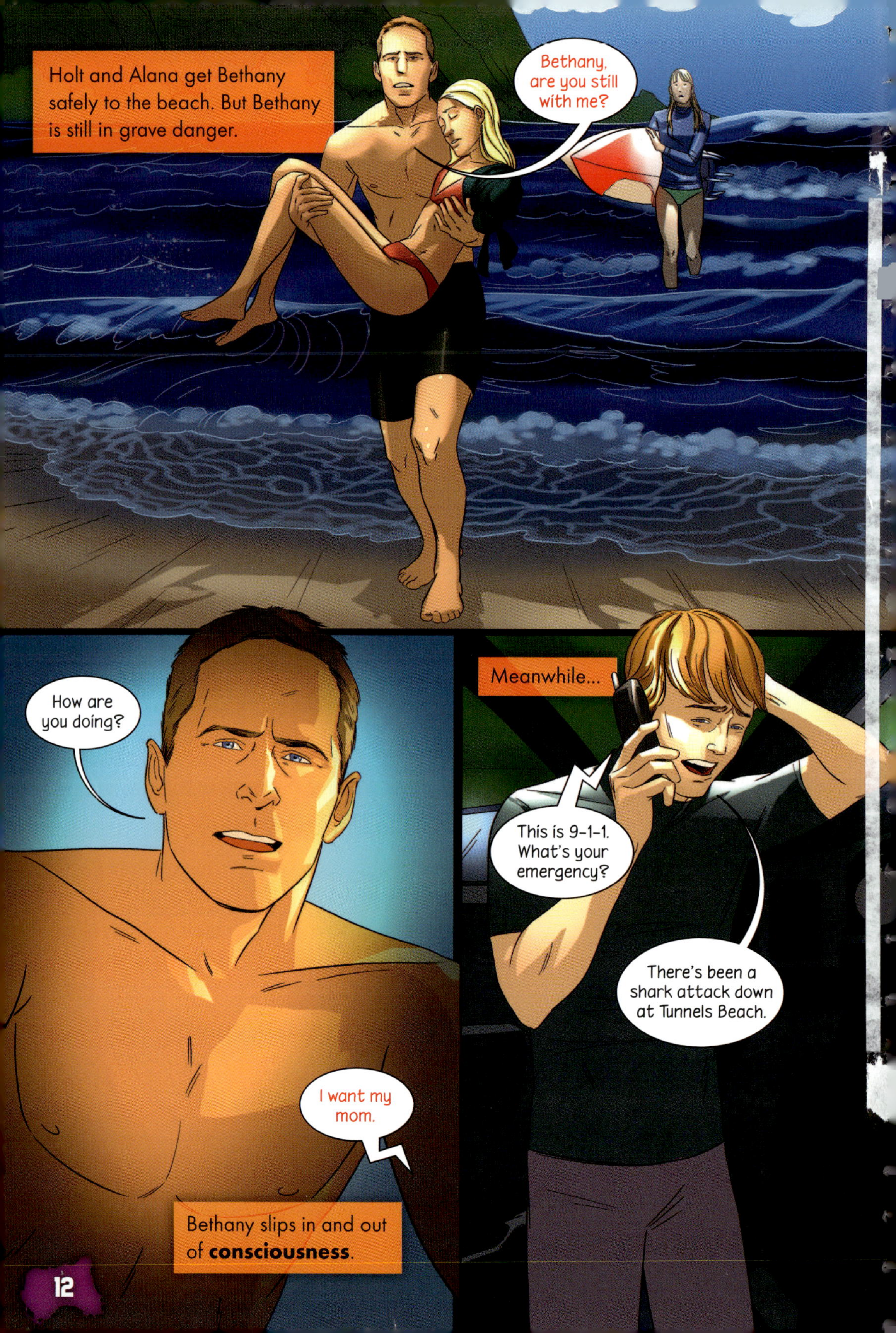
Holt and Alana get Bethany safely to the beach. But Bethany is still in grave danger.
Bethany, are you still with me?
How are you doing?
I want my mom.
Bethany slips in and out of **consciousness**.
Meanwhile...
This is 9-1-1. What's your emergency?
There's been a shark attack down at Tunnels Beach.

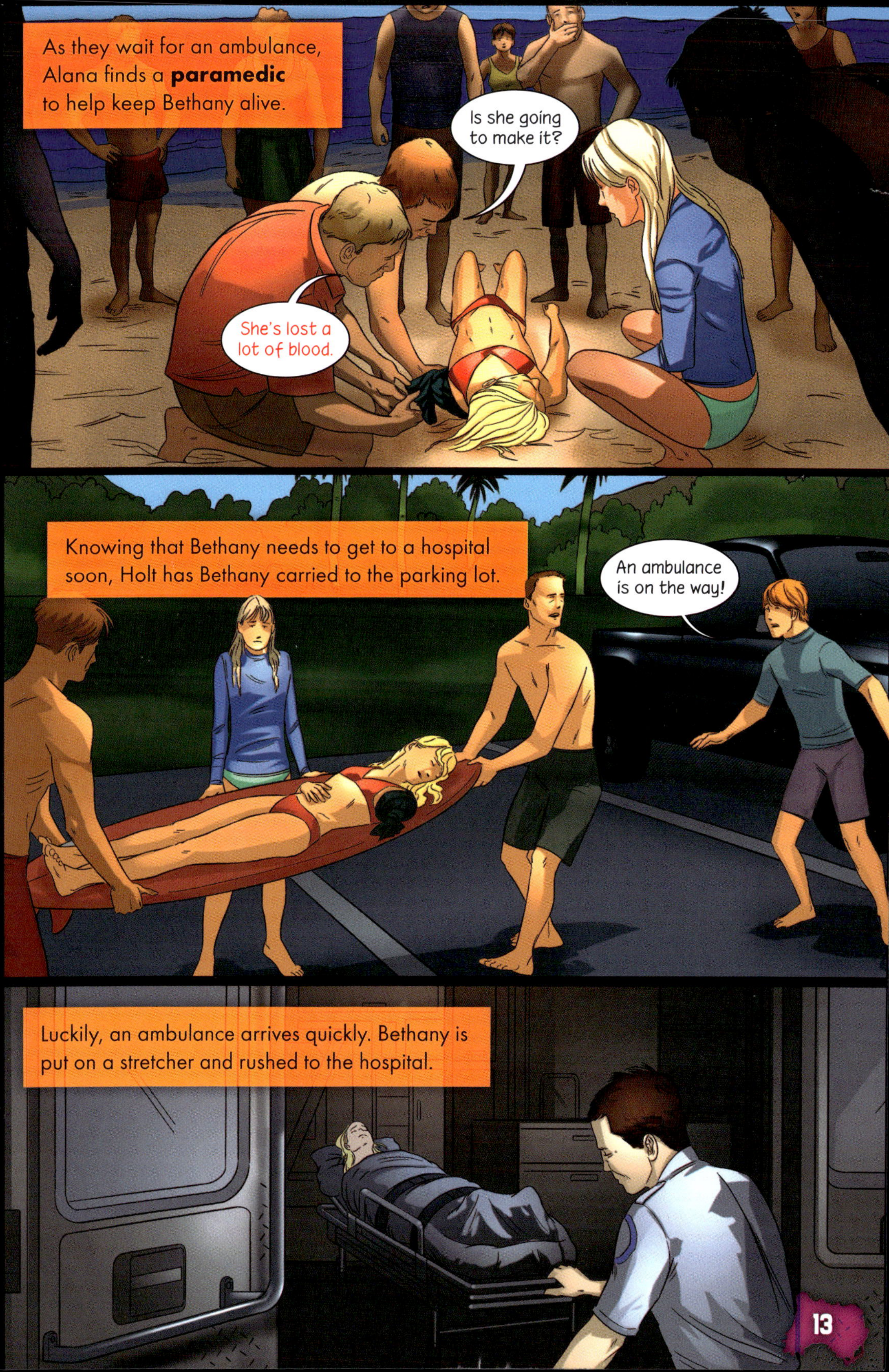
As they wait for an ambulance, Alana finds a **paramedic** to help keep Bethany alive.
Is she going to make it?
She's lost a lot of blood.
Knowing that Bethany needs to get to a hospital soon, Holt has Bethany carried to the parking lot.
An ambulance is on the way!
Luckily, an ambulance arrives quickly. Bethany is put on a stretcher and rushed to the hospital.

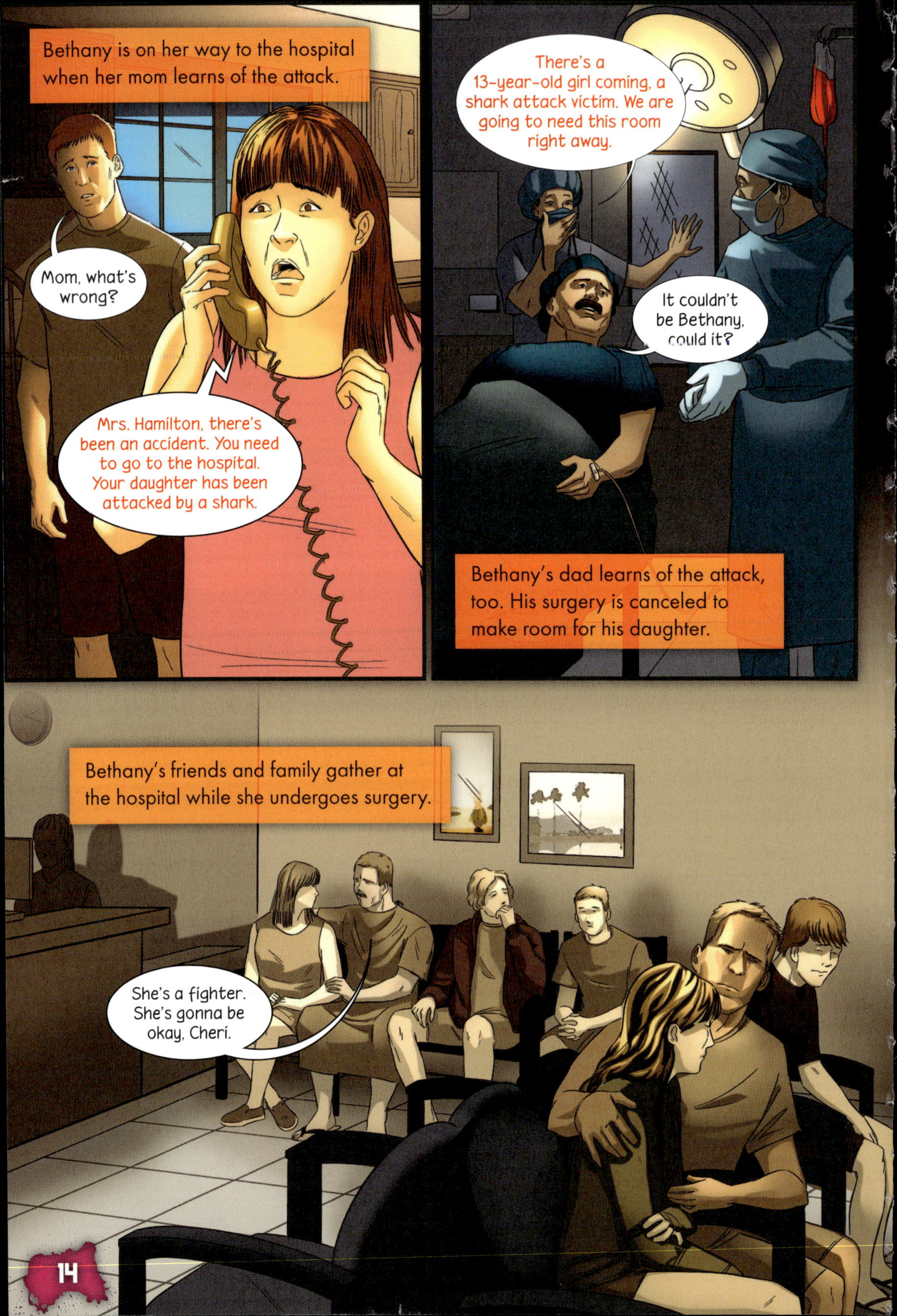
Bethany is on her way to the hospital when her mom learns of the attack.
Mom, what's wrong?
Mrs. Hamilton, there's been an accident. You need to go to the hospital. Your daughter has been attacked by a shark.
There's a 13-year-old girl coming, a shark attack victim. We are going to need this room right away.
It couldn't be Bethany, could it?
Bethany's dad learns of the attack, too. His surgery is canceled to make room for his daughter.
Bethany's friends and family gather at the hospital while she undergoes surgery.
She's a fighter. She's gonna be okay, Cheri.

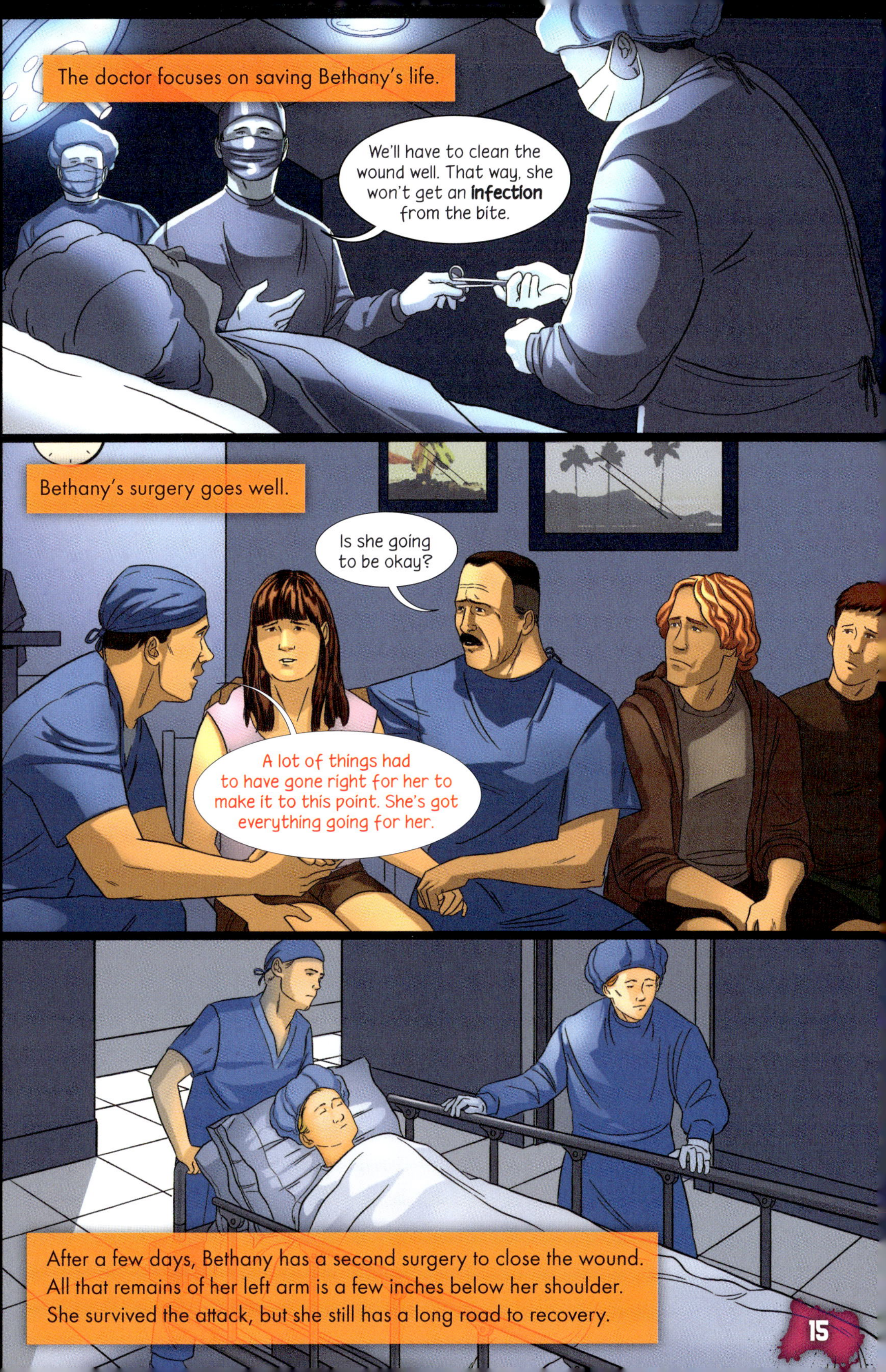

The doctor focuses on saving Bethany's life.
We'll have to clean the wound well. That way, she won't get an **infection** from the bite.
Bethany's surgery goes well.
Is she going to be okay?
A lot of things had to have gone right for her to make it to this point. She's got everything going for her.
After a few days, Bethany has a second surgery to close the wound. All that remains of her left arm is a few inches below her shoulder. She survived the attack, but she still has a long road to recovery.

THE ROAD TO RECOVERY

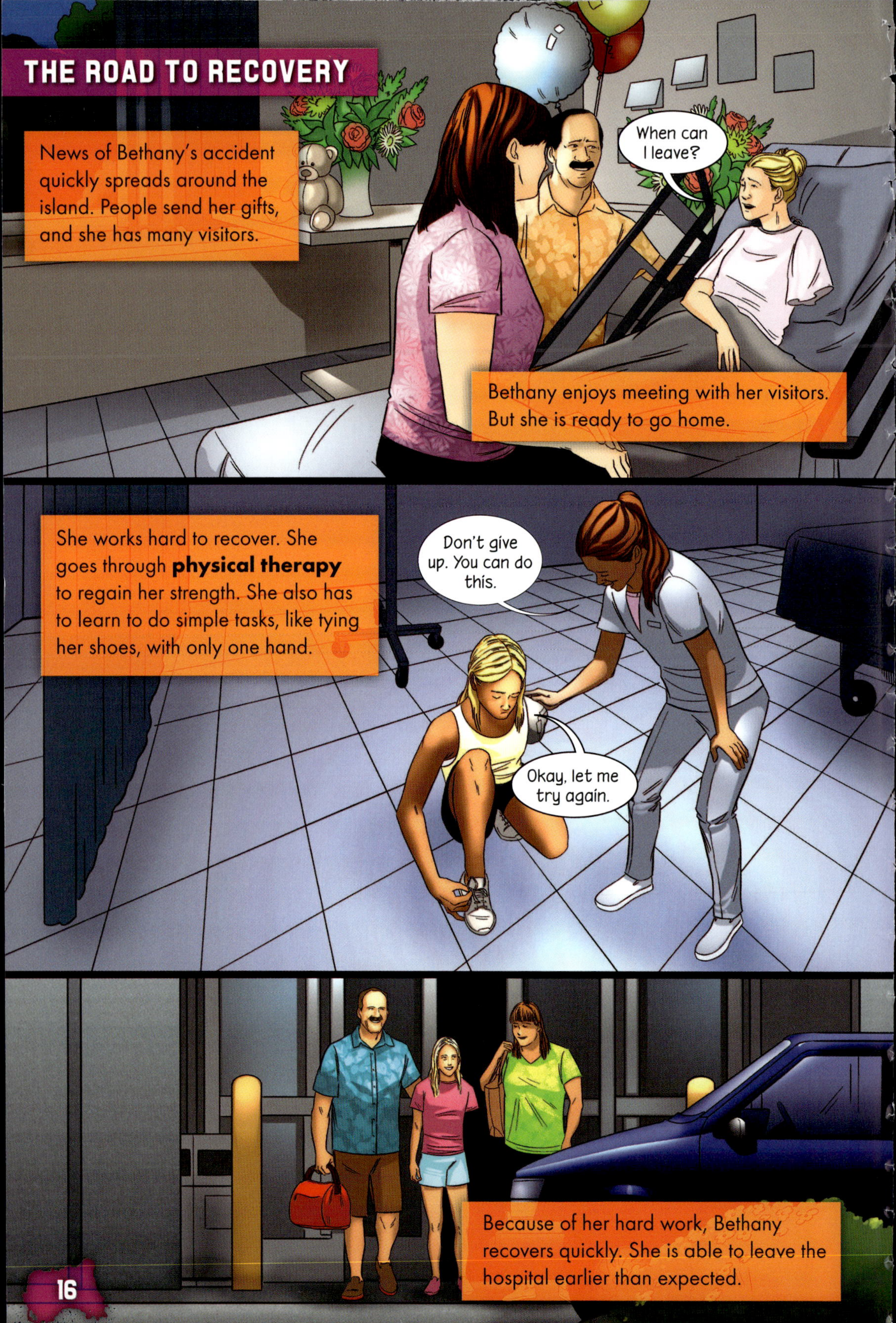
News of Bethany's accident quickly spreads around the island. People send her gifts, and she has many visitors.
When can I leave?
Bethany enjoys meeting with her visitors. But she is ready to go home.
She works hard to recover. She goes through **physical therapy** to regain her strength. She also has to learn to do simple tasks, like tying her shoes, with only one hand.
Don't give up. You can do this.
Okay, let me try again.
Because of her hard work, Bethany recovers quickly. She is able to leave the hospital earlier than expected.

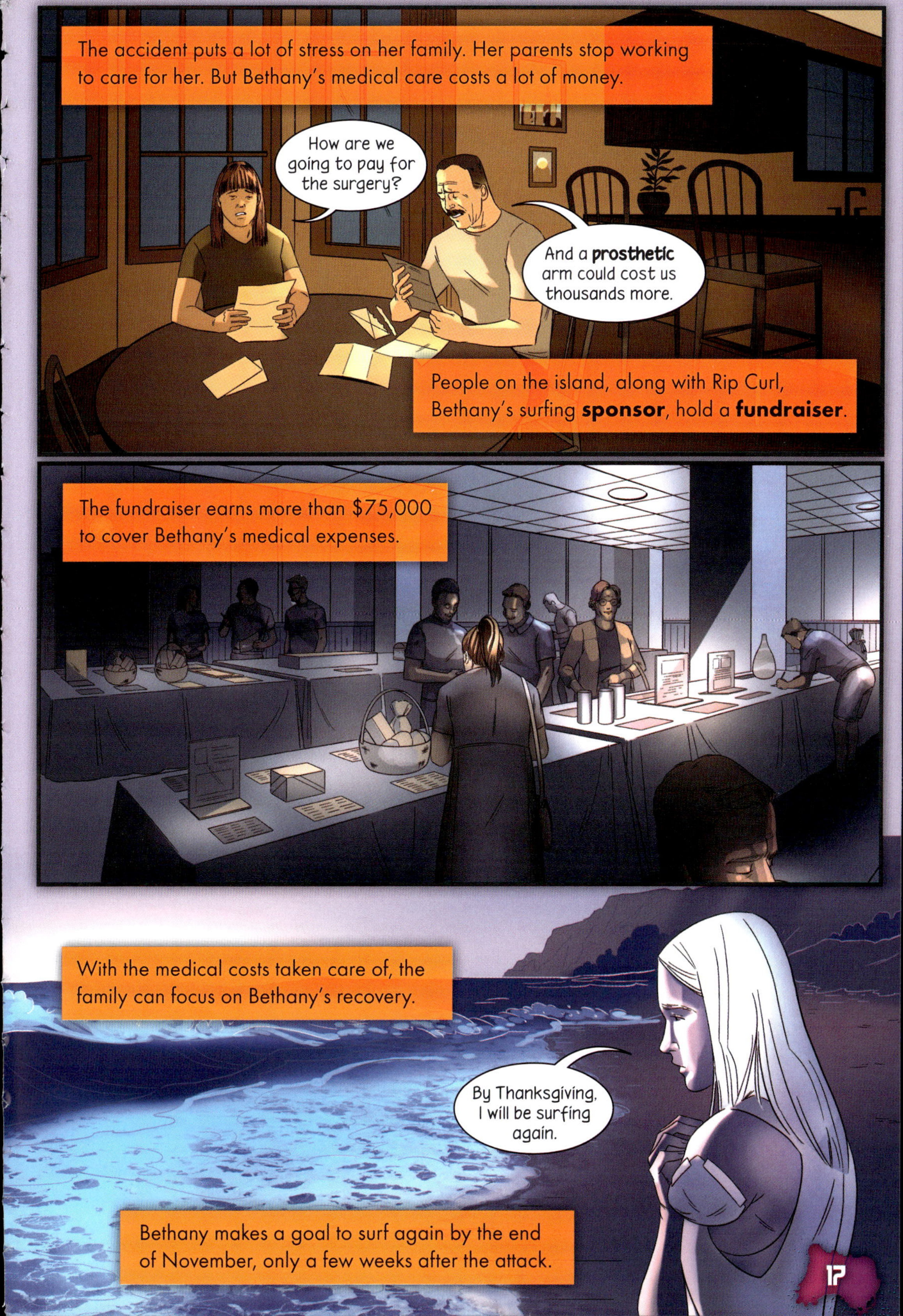
The accident puts a lot of stress on her family. Her parents stop working to care for her. But Bethany's medical care costs a lot of money.
How are we going to pay for the surgery?
And a **prosthetic** arm could cost us thousands more.
People on the island, along with Rip Curl, Bethany's surfing **sponsor**, hold a **fundraiser**.
The fundraiser earns more than $75,000 to cover Bethany's medical expenses.
With the medical costs taken care of, the family can focus on Bethany's recovery.
By Thanksgiving, I will be surfing again.
Bethany makes a goal to surf again by the end of November, only a few weeks after the attack.

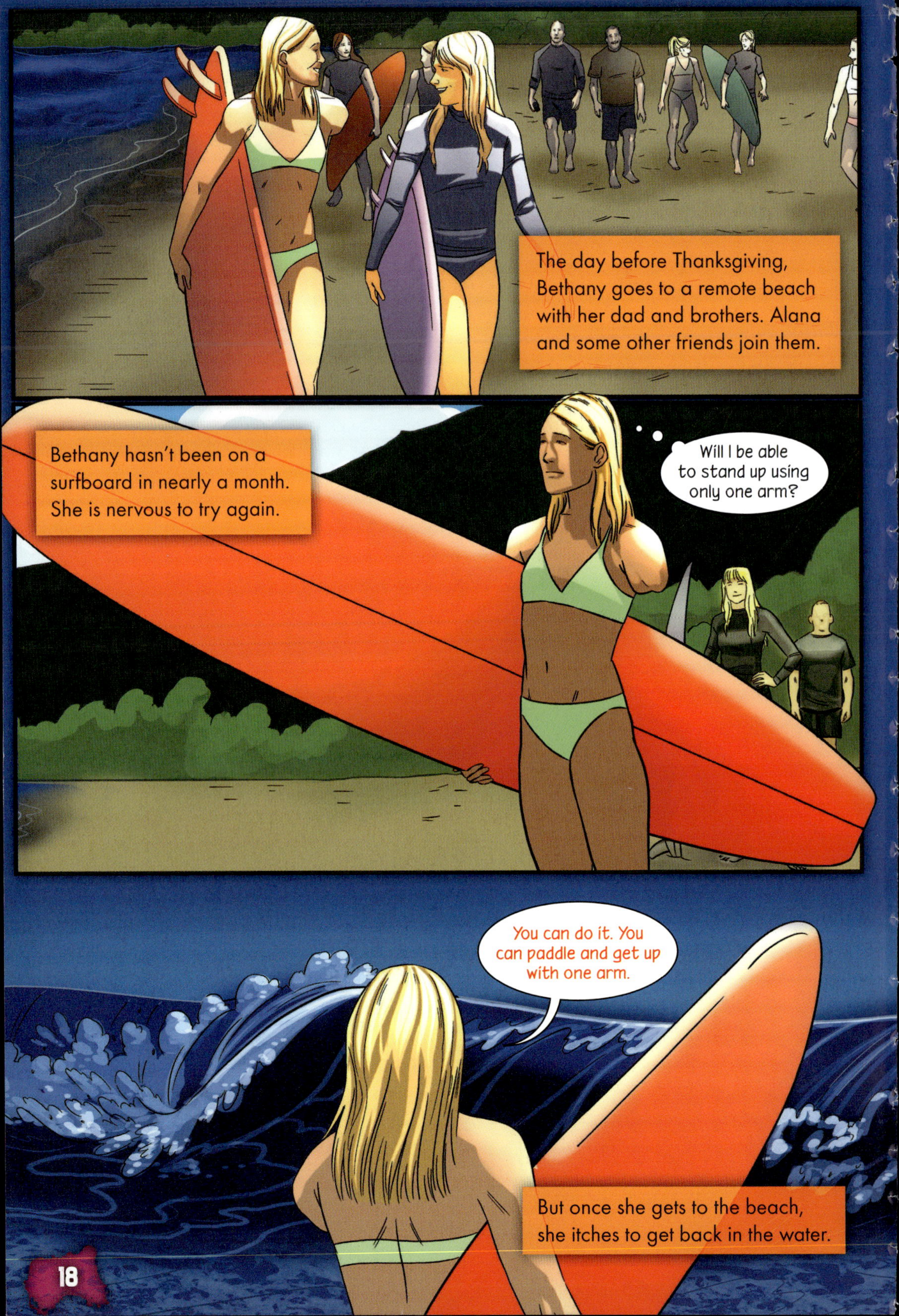

The day before Thanksgiving, Bethany goes to a remote beach with her dad and brothers. Alana and some other friends join them.
Bethany hasn't been on a surfboard in nearly a month. She is nervous to try again.
Will I be able to stand up using only one arm?
You can do it. You can paddle and get up with one arm.
But once she gets to the beach, she itches to get back in the water.

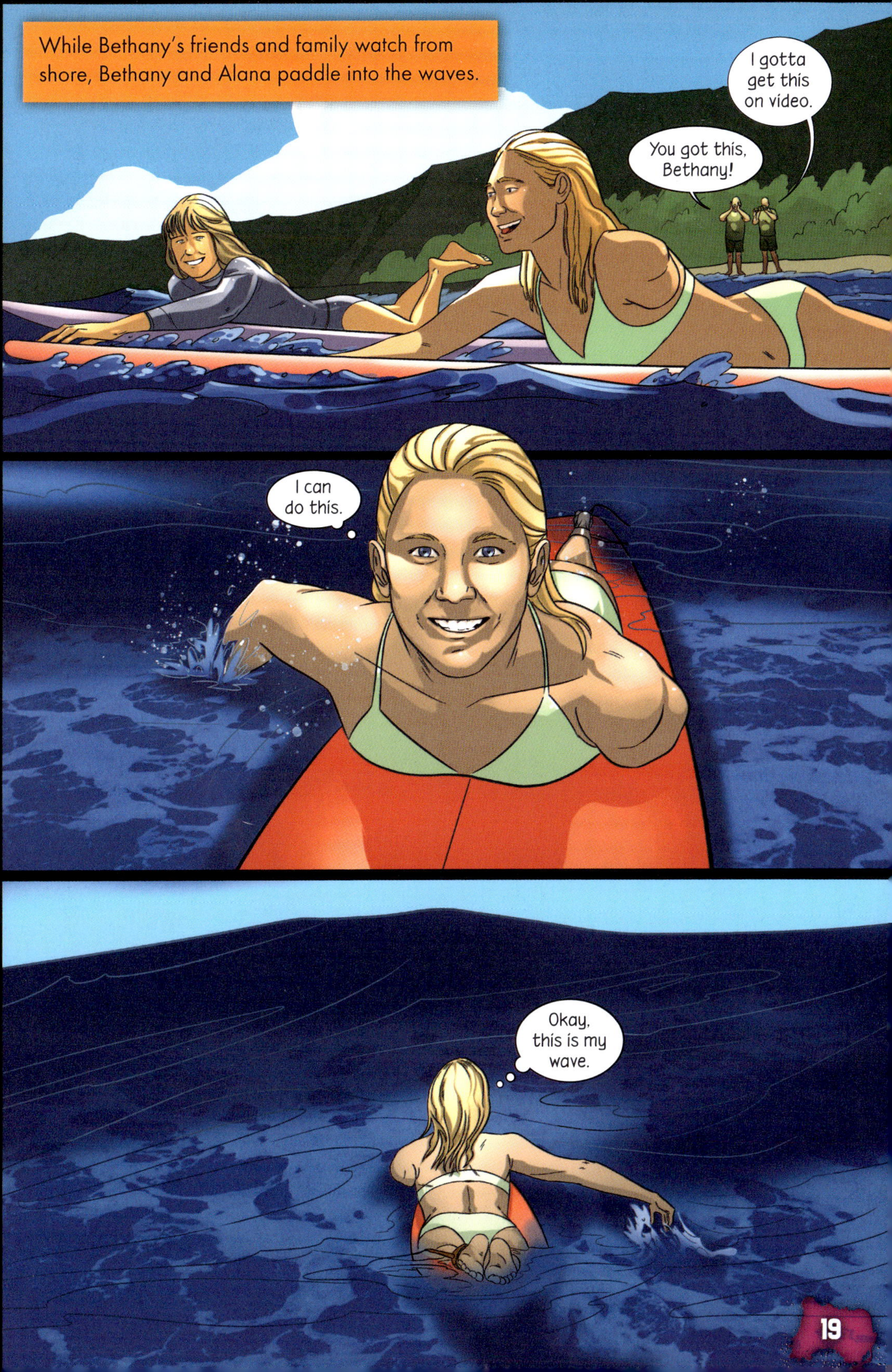
While Bethany's friends and family watch from shore, Bethany and Alana paddle into the waves.
I gotta get this on video.
You got this, Bethany!
I can do this.
Okay, this is my wave.

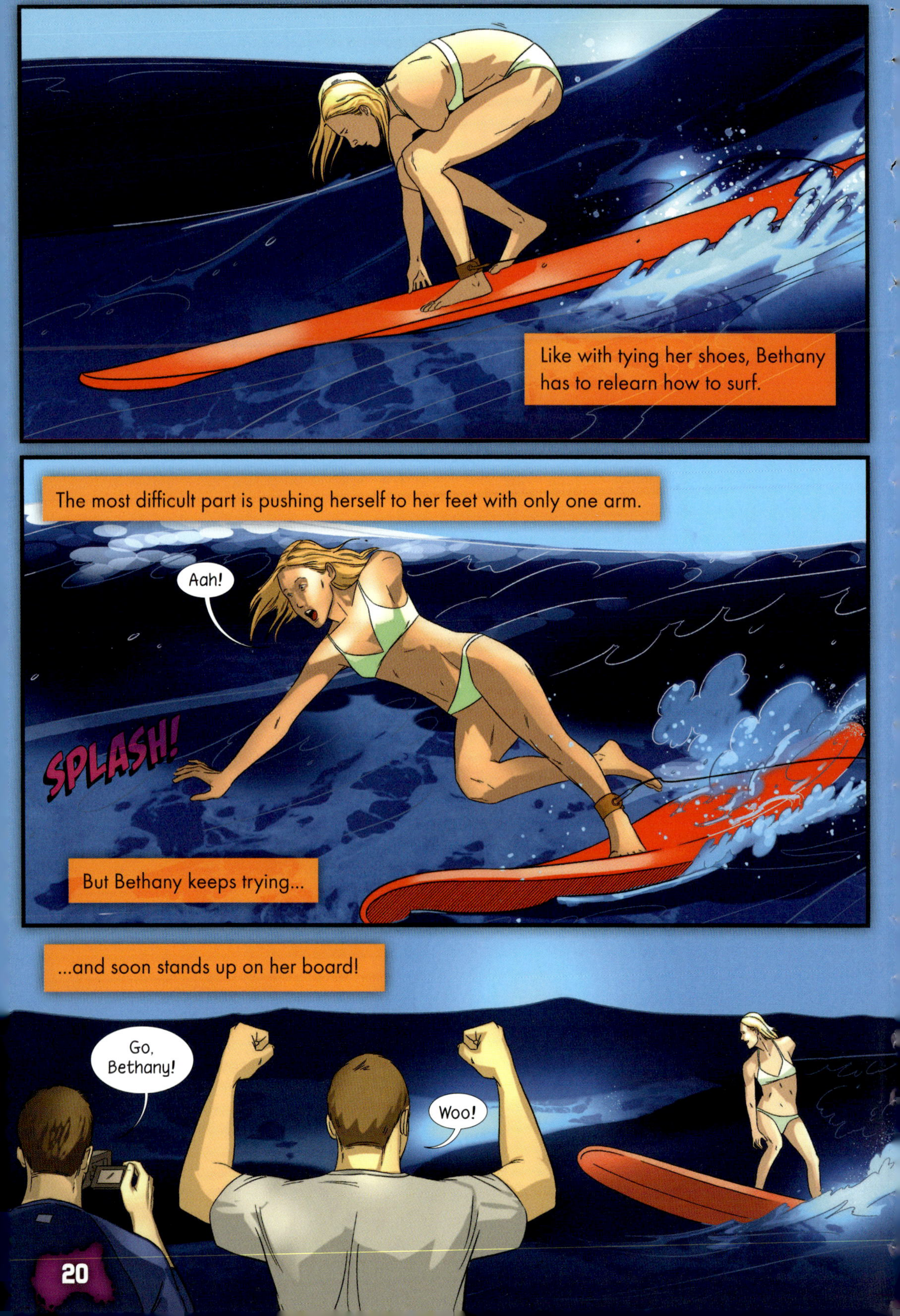
Like with tying her shoes, Bethany has to relearn how to surf.
The most difficult part is pushing herself to her feet with only one arm.
Aah!
SPLASH!
But Bethany keeps trying...
...and soon stands up on her board!
Go, Bethany!
Woo!

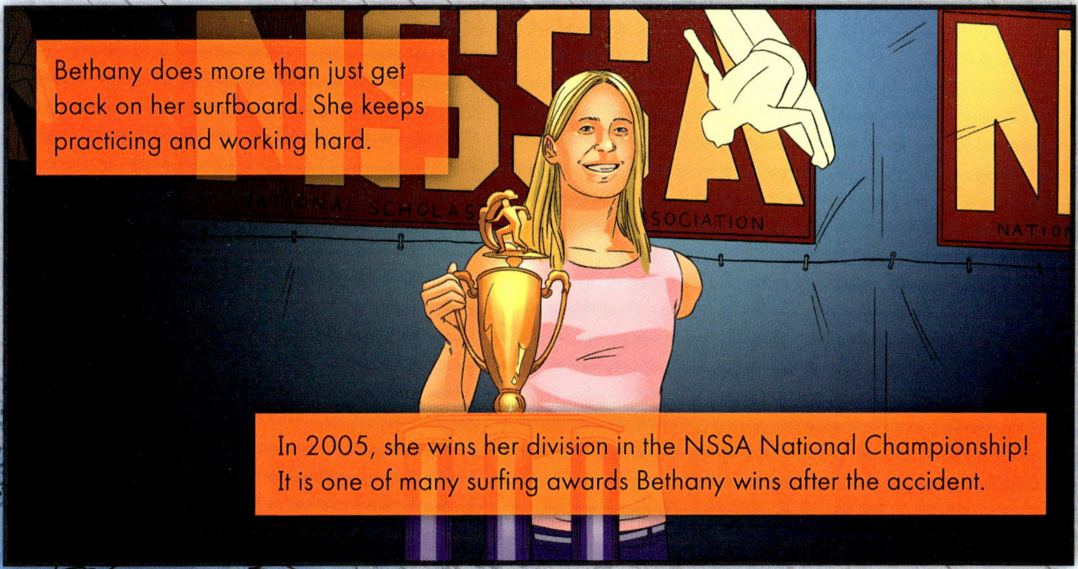
Bethany does more than just get back on her surfboard. She keeps practicing and working hard.
In 2005, she wins her division in the NSSA National Championship! It is one of many surfing awards Bethany wins after the accident.

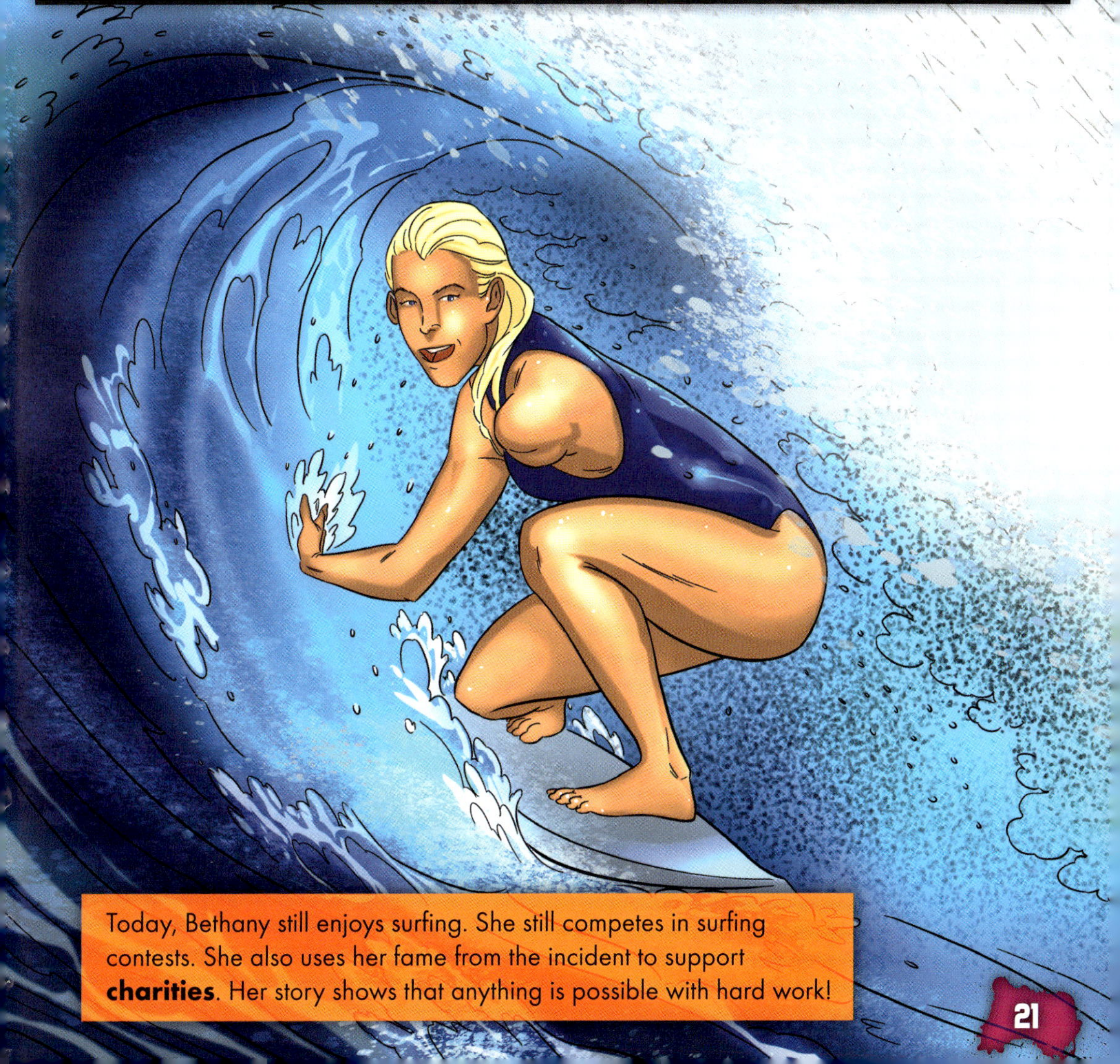
Today, Bethany still enjoys surfing. She still competes in surfing contests. She also uses her fame from the incident to support **charities**. Her story shows that anything is possible with hard work!

MORE ABOUT BETHANY HAMILTON

- After the shark attack, Bethany appeared on many TV talk shows, including *The Ellen DeGeneres Show* and *The Oprah Winfrey Show*.
- A movie has been made about Bethany's accident. *Soul Surfer* was released in 2011.
- The shark that attacked Bethany was caught soon after the incident. It weighed up to 1,800 pounds (816 kilograms).

BETHANY HAMILTON TIMELINE

October 31, 2003
Bethany is attacked by a shark while surfing

November 5, 2003
Bethany is released from the hospital

November 26, 2003
Bethany gets back on her surfboard for the first time since her accident

June 30, 2005
Bethany wins her division in the NSSA National Championship

BETHANY HAMILTON MAP

PAUAEAKA BEACH
TUNNELS BEACH
LIHUE (BETHANY'S HOMETOWN)
KAUAI
HAWAII

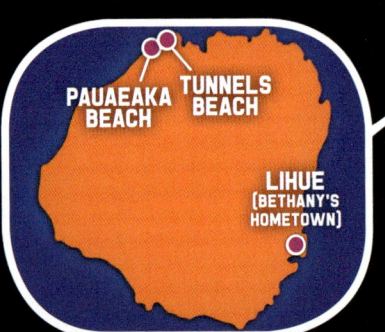

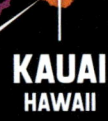

GLOSSARY

charities—organizations that raise money to help those in need

consciousness—the state of being awake and alert

currents—parts of a body of water that continuously move in a certain direction

fundraiser—an event held to raise money for something

infection—the presence of germs in a person's body, which can lead to sickness

paramedic—a person trained in providing emergency medical care

physical therapy—treatment that improves movement after a disease or injury

prosthetic—related to the human-made devices that replace or change missing or damaged body parts

rash guard—a shirt surfers wear to protect their skin from the sun, sand, and rubbing on their surfboards

reefs—ridges of sand, rock, or coral that are found in shallow ocean waters

sponsor—a person or company who gives money to support someone

TO LEARN MORE

AT THE LIBRARY

Harris, Tim. *Predator and Prey: How Sharks and Other Fish Attack!* New York, N.Y.: Hachette, 2021.

Marsico, Katie. *Surviving a Shark Attack: Bethany Hamilton.* Minneapolis, Minn.: Lerner Publications, 2019.

Nixon, Madeline. *Tiger Shark.* New York, N.Y.: AV2, 2019.

ON THE WEB

Factsurfer.com gives you a safe, fun way to find more information.

1. Go to www.factsurfer.com
2. Enter "Bethany Hamilton" into the search box and click 🔍.
3. Select your book cover to see a list of related content.

INDEX

Blanchard, Alana, 6, 7, 8, 10, 11, 12, 13, 18, 19
Blanchard, Byron, 6, 8, 11, 12, 13
Blanchard, Holt, 6, 8, 10, 11, 12, 13
charities, 21
contests, 4, 21
fundraiser, 17
Hamilton, Cheri, 4, 5, 6, 14, 17
Hamilton, Noah, 5, 14, 18, 19, 20
Hamilton, Timmy, 5, 18
Hamilton, Tom, 4, 5, 14, 15, 17, 18, 19, 20

historical quotes, 5, 6, 10, 11, 12, 13, 14, 15, 18
Kauai, Hawaii, 4, 6, 16, 17
map, 22
National Scholastic Surfing Association, 4, 21
Pauaeaka, 5, 6
recovery, 15, 16, 17, 18, 19, 20
Rip Curl, 17
shark, 8, 9, 10, 12, 14
timeline, 22
Tunnels Beach, 6, 7, 12

24